PRINCE 2: An Outline

London: The Stationery Office

Central Computer and Telecommunications Agency

© Crown Copyright 1997. Published for the Central Computer and Telecommunications Agency under licence from the Controller of Her Majesty s Stationery Office.

Applications for reproduction should be made in writing to the Copyright Unit, Her Majesty s Stationery Office, St Clements House, 2-16 Colegate, Norwich, NR3 1BQ

PRINCE ® is a registered trade mark of CCTA

The right of Colin Bentley to be identified as Author of this Work has been asserted in accordance with the Copyright, Designs and Patents Act 1988

Fourth impression 2000

ISBN 0 11 330854 X

For further information on CCTA products please contact:

CCTA Library
Rosebery Court
St Andrews Business Park
Norwich
NR7 OH5
Tel. 01603 704930

Contents

List of Figures

1. Introduction

1.1 Background

PRINCE 2 (**PR**ojects **IN** Controlled Environments) is a structured set of components, techniques and processes designed for managing any type or size of project.

It has its origins in the PROMPT II method, devised in 1975 by Simpact Systems Ltd. This was enhanced by the CCTA and was re-launched as PRINCE in 1989. A fully revised and updated version, PRINCE 2 was launched in October 1996.

PRINCE 2 is the recommended method for use in government organisations. The method is also successfully used by many private sector organisations. PRINCE 2 is owned by CCTA, the Central Computer and Telecommunications Agency.

1.2 Purpose

The purpose of this volume is to provide an introduction to the PRINCE 2 project management method. The volume aims to describe, in a concise and readable form, all the elements of the method and to discuss the underlying rationale of the method. Full details of the method can be found in the PRINCE 2 manual, published by The Stationery Office.

1.3 Readership

The volume is intended for a number of groups; firstly anyone interested in knowing about the method, but not yet ready to study the manual. It will also be of interest to people appointed to play a part in a project being run under PRINCE 2, either before looking at the manual or before undertaking any PRINCE 2 training.

The volume may also be found useful by people who have worked in or with PRINCE 2 projects in specific roles but feel the need to widen their understanding of the method as a whole.

Last but not least, the volume will be useful to those who know the original version of PRINCE and wish to find out what changes have been made to the method.

1.4 Why use PRINCE 2

In broadest terms, a project is a managed collection of activities to bring about a desired change. PRINCE 2 provides a framework whereby a bridge between a current state of affairs and a planned future state may be constructed. Once the planned state has been reached, the bridge will have served its purpose and is dismantled. All projects are thus finite; they end when they have served their purpose.

For a variety of reasons projects are often not well managed by normal line management, which is more concerned with maintaining continuity. Consequently, a dedicated team needs to be established to manage and carry out each project. At the end of the project this project team, like the project itself, is dismantled.

Although every project is technically unique in some way, all projects share common management issues and problems. A common approach to project management - a project management method - avoids the need to devise a specific approach for each project.

PRINCE 2 is a method for the management of any type or size of project. It is flexible and based on common sense. The fundamental principles can be applied to even the smallest projects.

PRINCE 2 focuses attention on products rather than activities, ensuring that the organisation gets what it wants, providing more reliable estimates of time and cost initially and more realistic and objective judgements of progress subsequently.

Quality is seen as a necessary and integral part of project work. The quality expectations are established at the outset and as the need for a product is identified, criteria are defined by which the quality of that product will be judged. The standards to be used in the construction of products, the inspection methods and responsibilities are an integral part of plans at all levels.

One view which can be taken of quality is the value of a project's end product to the business. PRINCE 2 provides a framework in which the needs of the business should never be overlooked. In particular, PRINCE 2 requires the development of a viable business case for a project at its outset and ensures that the business case is periodically reconsidered throughout development.

PRINCE 2 recognises that the management of risk is one of the most important elements of project management and builds this in to the key events throughout a project.

Finally, because PRINCE 2 is in the public domain, users of the method have an unrivalled choice of supplier when looking for training, consultancy support or support tools.

A list of accredited suppliers of training and consultancy can be obtained from the APM Group Ltd, with whom the CCTA work in the promotion of PRINCE 2.

They can be reached by the following means:

Telephone: 01494 452450

Fax: 01494 459559

Email: info@apmgroup.co.uk

Address: 7-8 Queen Square, High Wycombe, Buckinghamshire HP11 2BP

The following publications are available from The Stationery Office (for addresses see back cover):

PRINCE 2   ISBN 0 11 330685 7

PRINCE 2 Pocketbook   ISBN 0 11 330853 1

2. An Overview of PRINCE 2

2.1   Introduction

Organisations are becoming increasingly aware of the opportunities for adopting a "project" approach to the way in which they address the creation and delivery of new business products or implement any change. They are also increasingly aware of the benefits which a single, common, structured approach to project management can bring.

PRINCE 2 gives:

- controlled management of change by the business in terms of investment and return on investment

- active involvement of the users of the final product throughout its development to ensure the business product will meet the functional, environmental, service and management requirements of the users

- more efficient control of development resources,

which is how its users derive the benefits mentioned in Chapter 1.

To derive these benefits, organisations require a project management method which will meet and fit their particular needs.

Figure 1: Components and Processes

A key concept of the method is that it firmly distinguishes the management of the development process from the development process itself.

PRINCE 2 has a process-based approach to project management. The processes define the management activities to be carried out during the project. In addition, PRINCE 2 describes a number of components which are applied within the appropriate activities. Figure 1 shows the components positioned around the central process model.

2.2 **The Components**

The components of PRINCE 2 are:

Organisation

A definition of the roles, responsibilities and relationships of all staff involved in the project.

Planning

An approach to planning based on products rather than activities and the use of this approach for the benefit of different levels of management.

Controls

A set of controls which facilitate the provision of key decision-making information, allowing the organisation to pre-empt problems and make decisions on problem resolution.

Stages

An approach to defining the "shape" of a project to promote sound business control.

Management of Risk

Risk is a major factor to be considered during the life of a project. PRINCE 2 defines the key points when risks should be reviewed, outlines an approach to the management of project risk, and provides guidance on the "ownership" of risks.

Quality in a Project Environment

PRINCE 2 recognises the importance of quality and incorporates a quality approach to the management and technical processes.

Configuration Management

There are many methods of configuration management available. PRINCE 2 does not attempt to invent a new one, but defines the essential facilities and information requirements for a configuration management method and how it should link with other PRINCE 2 components and techniques.

Change Control

PRINCE 2 emphasises the need for change control and this is enforced with a change control technique plus identification of the processes which apply the change control.

2.3 The Processes

The steps of project management are described in eight processes, shown in Figure 2. This is a summary of the processes.

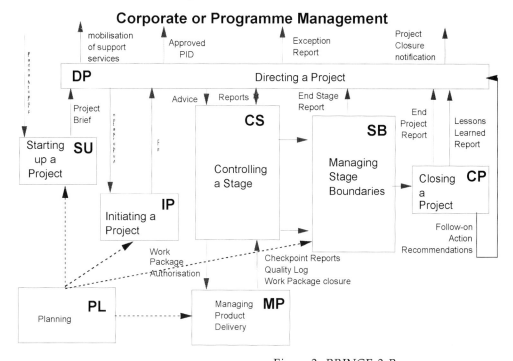

Figure 2: PRINCE 2 Processes

Any project run under PRINCE 2 will need to address each of these processes **in some form**. However, the key to successful use of the process model is in tailoring it to the needs of the individual project. Each process should be approached with the question "How extensively should this process be applied on this project?"

2.3.1 Directing a Project (DP)

This process is aimed at the senior management team responsible for the project, the key decision makers. These are very busy people and should be involved in only the decision-making process. PRINCE 2 helps them achieve this by adopting the philosophy of "management by exception". The DP process covers the steps to be taken by this senior management team (the Project Board) throughout the project from start-up to project closure and has five major steps:

- authorising the preparation of a project plan and business case for the project

- approving the project go-ahead

- checking that the project remains justifiable at key points in the project life cycle

- monitoring progress and giving advice as required

- ensuring that the project comes to a controlled close.

2.3.2	Starting Up a Project (SU)	This is intended to be a very short pre-project process with four objectives:

- ensure that the aims of the project are known

- design and appoint the Project Management Team

- decide on the approach which will be taken within the project to provide a solution

- plan the work needed to draw up the PRINCE 2 "contract" between customer and supplier.

2.3.3	Initiating a Project (IP)	This process prepares the information on whether there is sufficient justification to proceed with the project, establishes a sound management basis for the project and creates a detailed plan for as much of the project as management are in a position to authorise. The management product created is the Project Initiation Document, the baseline against which progress and success will be measured.
2.3.4	Controlling a Stage (CS)	This process describes the monitoring and control activities of the Project Manager involved in ensuring that a stage stays on course and reacts to unexpected events. The process forms the core of the Project Manager's effort on the project, being the process which handles day-to-day management of the project development activity.

Throughout a stage there will be many cycles of:

- authorising work to be done

- gathering progress information about that work

- watching for changes

- reviewing the situation

- reporting

- taking any necessary action.

The process covers these activities, together with the ongoing work of risk management and change control.

2.3.5	Managing Product Delivery (MP)	This process provides a control mechanism so that the Project Manager and specialist teams can agree details of the work required. This is particularly important where one or more teams are from third party suppliers not adopting PRINCE 2. The work agreed between the Project Manager and the Team Manager, including target dates, quality and reporting requirements, is called a work package.

The process covers:

- making sure that work allocated to the team is authorised and agreed

- planning the team work

- ensuring that the work is done

- ensuring that products meet the agreed quality criteria

- reporting on progress and quality to the Project Manager

- obtaining acceptance of the finished products.

2.3.6	Managing Stage Boundaries (SB)	The objectives of this process are to:

- plan the next stage

- update the project plan

- update the business case

- update the risk assessment

- report on the outcome and performance of the stage which has just ended

- obtain Project Board approval to move into the next stage.

If the Project Board requests the Project Manager to produce an exception plan (see "Controls" for an explanation), this process also covers the steps needed for that.

2.3.7	Closing a Project (CP)	The process covers the Project Manager's work to request Project Board permission to close the project either at its natural end or at a premature close requested by the Project Board. The objectives are to:

- note the extent to which the objectives set out at the start of the project have been met

- confirm the customer's satisfaction with the products

- confirm that maintenance and support arrangements are in place (where appropriate)

- make any recommendations for follow-on actions

- ensure that all lessons learned during the project are annotated for the benefit of future projects

- report on whether the project management activity itself has been a success or not

- prepare a plan to check on achievement of the product's claimed benefits.

2.3.8   Planning (PL)

Planning is a repeatable process, used by the other processes whenever a plan is required. The process makes use of the PRINCE 2 product-based planning technique and covers:

- designing the plan

- defining and analysing the plan's products

- identifying the necessary activities and dependencies

- estimating the effort required

- scheduling resources

- analysing the risks

- adding text to describe the plan, its assumptions and the quality steps.

3. Organisation

PRINCE 2 provides a model organisation for undertaking projects. This model organisation can be tailored to meet the requirements of a specific project. The flexibility of PRINCE 2 is achieved by specifying a set of roles with responsibilities and activities. Organisations must then decide how these roles should be mapped onto available staff for each project. In a small project, one person may take on a number of roles. Conversely, in large projects a particular role may be so large that it needs to be shared between a number of people. The various roles are outlined below with brief examples of how they might be applied to various sizes and types of project.

3.1 Fundamental Principles

Good project management practice requires the fulfilment of a number of roles which are generic and fairly well defined on any project. For a project to be successful it is important to decide at the outset who is doing what.

A project needs a different organisation structure to line management. A project needs to be more flexible and is likely to require a broad base of skills for a comparatively short period of time. It is normally cross-functional, an involved partnership.

A project organisation combines people who are working full-time on the project with others who have to divide their time between the project and other permanent duties. The Project Manager will have direct management control over some of the project staff, but may also have to direct staff who report to another manager.

The management priorities and needs of those with a problem to be solved will very often be different from that of those providing the solution. They will have different priorities, different interests to protect, but in some way they must be united in the common aims of the project. The management level which will make the decisions and the commitments on behalf of their interests is too busy to be involved on a day-to-day basis with the project. But most projects need day-to-day management if they are to be successful. The PRINCE 2 project organisation structure shown in Figure 3 meets all these needs.

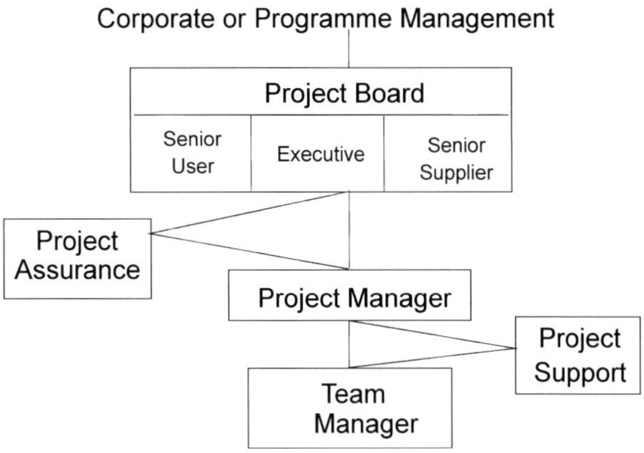

Corporate or Programme Management

```
                    ┌─────────────────────────────────┐
                    │          Project Board           │
                    ├──────────┬───────────┬──────────┤
                    │  Senior  │ Executive │  Senior  │
                    │   User   │           │ Supplier │
                    └──────────┴───────────┴──────────┘

        ┌──────────────┐              ┌─────────────────┐
        │   Project    │              │ Project Manager │
        │  Assurance   │              └─────────────────┘
        └──────────────┘                                    ┌──────────┐
                              ┌───────────────┐             │ Project  │
                              │     Team      │             │ Support  │
                              │    Manager    │             └──────────┘
                              └───────────────┘
```

Figure 3: The PRINCE 2 Organisation Structure

The PRINCE 2 project management structure is based on a customer/supplier environment. The structure assumes that there will be a customer who will specify the desired outcome, make use of the outcome and probably pay for the project, and a (prime) supplier who will provide the resources and skills to create that outcome. This assumption has a bearing on how the project is organised.

The customer and supplier may be part of the same corporate body or may be independent of each other.

3.1.1 Project Board

The Project Board represents the Business, User and Supplier interests of the project. The Project Board members must have managerial authority because they are the decision-makers and responsible for the commitment of resources to the project, such as personnel, cash and equipment. No one should be a Project Board member if they cannot make the necessary commitments and decisions.

The level of manager required will depend on such factors as the budget and importance of the project. Their Project Board responsibilities will be in addition to their normal work, which makes it important that they are kept regularly informed, and only asked for joint decision-making at a small number of key points in the project.

The Project Board consists of three roles:

- Executive
- Senior User
- Senior Supplier.

These roles should ideally be assigned to individuals who can stay with the project throughout its life.

The Project Board is appointed to provide overall direction and management of the project. The Project Board is accountable for the success of the project, and has responsibility and authority for the project within the remit (the Project Mandate) set by corporate or programme management.

The Project Board approves the project and stage plans and authorises any major deviation from agreed stage plans. It ensures that required resources are committed and arbitrates on any conflicts within the project or between the project and external bodies. In addition, it approves the appointment and responsibilities of the Project Manager.

The Project Board is accountable and responsible for assurance that the project remains on course to deliver products of the required quality to meet the business case defined in the Project Initiation Document. According to the size, complexity and risk of the project, the Project Board may choose to delegate some or all of this assurance work. Project assurance is discussed in 3.1.7.

The Project Board is the project's "voice" to the outside world and is responsible for any publicity or other dissemination of information about the project.

In a small project the roles of Executive and Senior User may be taken by the same person. Occasionally, where a manager is asking his or her own staff to develop a small project, all three Project Board roles may be taken by the same manager.

3.1.2   Executive

The Executive is ultimately accountable for the project, supported by the Senior User and Senior Supplier. The Executive has to ensure that the project is value for money and that there is a cost-conscious approach to the project, balancing the demands of business, user and supplier.

Throughout the project the Executive "owns" the business case.

| 3.1.3 | Senior User | The Senior User is accountable for making sure that what is produced is fit for purpose and for monitoring that the solution will meet user needs within the constraints of the business case. |

The role represents the interests of all those who will use the final product(s) of the project. The Senior User role commits user resources and monitors products against requirements. This role may require more than one person to cover all the user interests. For the sake of effectiveness the role should not be split between too many people.

| 3.1.4 | Senior Supplier | This role represents the interests of those designing, developing, facilitating, procuring, implementing, operating and maintaining the project products. The Senior Supplier role must have the authority to commit or acquire the required supplier resources. The Senior Supplier has responsibility for the supplier's business case. |

Where products are being supplied by one or more external bodies, the role may be filled by someone such as a company's contracts manager. Alternatively, more than one person may be required to represent a range of suppliers.

| 3.1.5 | Project Manager | The Project Manager manages the project on a day-to-day basis on behalf of the Project Board within the constraints laid down by that board. The role is normally filled by someone from the customer organisation. |

The Project Manager's prime responsibility is to ensure that the project produces the required products, to the required standard of quality and within the specified constraints of time and cost. The Project Manager is also responsible for the project producing a result which is capable of achieving the benefits defined in the Project Initiation Document.

| 3.1.6 | Team Manager | The use of this role is optional. The Project Manager may find that it is beneficial to delegate the authority and responsibility for planning the creation of certain products and managing a team of specialists to produce those products. There are many reasons why it may be decided to employ this role. Some of these are the size of the project, the particular specialist skills or knowledge needed for certain products, geographical |

location of some project members, and the preferences of the Project Board.

A Team Manager's prime responsibility is to ensure production of those products defined by the Project Manager to an appropriate quality, in a timescale and at a cost acceptable to the Project Manager. The Team Manager reports to and takes direction from the Project Manager.

3.1.7   Project Assurance

Project assurance is the independent monitoring of project progress on behalf of one or more members of the Project Board. It may be done by the Project Board members themselves or they may delegate some or all of their assurance responsibilities to others who have more time or more appropriate skills. Where assurance responsibilities are delegated, the Project Board member(s) still remain **accountable** for assurance.

The three major areas of assurance are:

- business (monitoring the business case, business risks and expenditure)

- technical (monitoring the use of standards and the quality of the products)

- user (monitoring that the end product continues to meet the user's specification throughout its development)

Project assurance monitors the work of the Project Manager, Team Managers and team members. Project assurance is independent of the Project Manager, therefore the Project Board cannot delegate its assurance responsibilities to the Project Manager.

3.1.8   Project Support

This is another optional set of roles, covering project administration, support tool expertise (such as planning and control tools), change control and configuration management. Below is a list of typical project support tasks. Depending on such factors as the project size and the abilities of the Project Manager, support may be needed to carry out some or all of these tasks:

- provide expertise in the planning and control tool(s) to be used

- collect actuals data and forecasts

- update plans

- administer change control
- set up and maintain project files
- establish a configuration management method for the project
- establish document control procedures
- administer the Quality Review process
- administer Project Board meetings.

4. Planning

4.1 What is a Plan?

A plan is a document, framed in accordance with a pre-defined scheme or method, describing **how**, **when** and **by whom** a specific target or set of targets are to be achieved.

4.2 Benefits of Planning

Effective planning identifies:

- whether the targets are achievable
- the resources needed to achieve the targets within a timeframe
- the activities needed to ensure that quality can be built in to the products
- the problems and risks associated with trying to achieve the targets and stay within the constraints.

Other benefits of planning include:

- avoiding muddle and ad hoc decisions
- helping the management team think ahead
- providing a yardstick against which progress can be measured
- distribution of a plan to all concerned which communicates what is to be done, how it is to be done, the allocation of responsibilities and how progress will be monitored and controlled
- gaining commitment from the contributors and recipients
- the setting of personal targets.

Without effective planning, the outcome of complex projects cannot be predicted in terms of scope, quality, risk, timescale and cost. Those involved in providing resources cannot optimise their operations. Poorly planned projects cause frustration, waste and re-work.

4.3 The PRINCE 2 Approach

The PRINCE 2 planning structure allows for a plan to be broken down into lower level plans containing more detail, but all plans have the same overall structure and are always referenced back to the planned requirements, including quality and benefits, before approval.

4.4   Levels of Plan

Activity durations and resource requirements become more difficult to estimate accurately, the further into the future they extend. Regardless of this problem, there is still a need to provide a provisional estimate of the duration and cost of the project as a whole in order to gain approval to proceed.

It is seldom desirable, or possible, to plan an entire project in detail at the start. The reasons for this include:

- uncertainty about the detailed nature of later elements of work

- a changing or uncertain environment

- risk factors which could change the situation

- difficulty in predicting resource availability well into the future

- difficulty in predicting business conditions in the future.

However, if the current elements of work are to be controlled, detailed plans containing firm estimates are needed for the realistically foreseeable future. For these reasons, plans need to be produced at different levels of scope and detail.

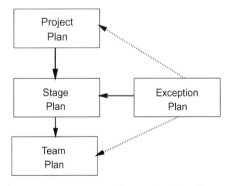

Figure 4: PRINCE 2 Plan Levels

Every PRINCE 2 project should have an initiation stage in which time is allocated to identify and agree the scope of the project and to plan it in terms of management, resourcing, deliverables, activities, quality and control. Time should also be allocated for the refinement of the business case. The initiation stage may or may not be formal, depending on the nature and complexity of the project. In addition, during the initiation stage and towards the end of every stage in the project except the last one, time should be allowed for planning the next stage in detail.

4.4.1   Project Plan

The project plan is mandatory. It provides the business case with project costs and is used by the Project Board as a baseline against which to monitor actual costs and project progress.

The project plan identifies key deliverables, resource requirements and the total costs. It also identifies major control points within the project, such as stage boundaries.

4.4.2   Stage Plan

For each stage identified in the project plan, a stage plan is required for the Project Manager's day-to-day control.

The stage plan is similar to the project plan in content, but each element will be broken down to the level of detail required to be an adequate basis for day-to-day control by the Project Manager. The validity of assumptions and risk analyses should be re-assessed for each stage, as these may have changed since they were previously considered, new risks may have arisen or become apparent when examined in more detail.

Each stage plan is finalised near the end of the previous stage. This approach should give more confidence in the plan because:

- the stage plan is produced close to the time when the planned events will take place

- the stage plan is for a much shorter duration than the project plan

- after the first stage the stage plan is developed with knowledge of the performance of earlier stages.

4.4.3   Exception Plans

When it is predicted that a plan will no longer finish within the agreed tolerances, an exception plan is produced to replace the remainder of that plan. An exception plan is prepared at the same level of detail as the plan it replaces. Most exception plans will be created to replace a stage or team plan, but the project plan may also need to be replaced. An exception plan picks up from the current stage or team plan actuals and continues to the end of the stage.

An exception plan has the same format as the plan which it replaces, but the text will cover why the exception plan is needed.

4.4.4   Team Plan

Team plans are **optional** and are used to break down activities into a lower level of tasks which are to produce one or more of the stage plan's products. They might be used for separate teams working in a stage, especially if those teams are from different skill groups, or work for single contractors. The Team Manager would use the team plan. The stage plan would be a summary of the various team plans.

The need for team plans will be determined by the size and complexity of the project and the number of people involved. If they are considered necessary, the plans are prepared in parallel with the stage plan.

4.5   What Are The Components of a Plan?

When asked to describe a plan, many people consider only its pictorial view. PRINCE 2 requires this to be supported by text. The diagrammatic representation of an acceptable PRINCE 2 plan should show:

- the products to be produced (the deliverables)

- the activities needed to create those deliverables

- what activities are needed to validate the quality of deliverables

- the resources and time needed for all activities (including quality control), and any need for people with specific skills

- the dependencies between activities

- external dependencies for the delivery of information, products or services

- when activities will occur

- the points at which progress will be monitored and controlled.

The statement of activities and breakdown of resource requirements must be backed up by text which explains to the reader:

- what the plan covers (e.g. delivery of specific products)

- the intended approach to implement the plan

- how adherence to it is to be monitored and controlled

- what management reports will be issued

- the quality plan

- the quality control methods and resources to be used

- any assumptions on which the plan is based

- any pre-requisites which must be in place on day one of the plan

- what risks there are which may prevent the plan being achieved and what measures should be taken to address these risks.

4.6   Product-based Planning

PRINCE 2 provides a product-based framework which can be applied to any project to give a logical sequence to the project's work. The use of this technique is recommended for all levels of plan required in a project. The technique is used by the "Planning" process (PL).

There are three steps to the product-based planning technique:

- producing a Product Breakdown Structure

- writing Product Descriptions

- producing a Product Flow Diagram.

4.6.1   Producing a Product Breakdown Structure

Breaking down a product into its constituent sub-products helps clarify and identify all necessary work for its creation.

This is the first step in PRINCE 2 product-based planning. The "product" is the end deliverable of the project and may be a tangible one such as a machine, a document or a piece of software, or it may be intangible, such as a culture change or a different organisation structure.

The objective is to identify the products or products, whether business need, management or quality, whose creation is the subject of the plan.

All the products of the plan are drawn up in a hierarchical structure, known as a Product Breakdown Structure. At the top of the chart is a single box which summarises the overall product of the plan, e.g. a new marketing strategy, a business plan, a new car, a computer system, a new employment policy.

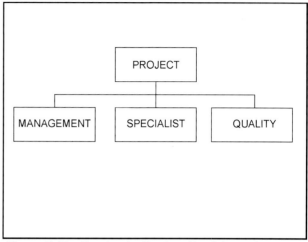

Figure 5: Top Levels of a Product Breakdown Structure

Below the top box are three boxes for the different types of project product. Each of these boxes is then decomposed into its major parts to form the next level of the structure. Each of these parts may be further decomposed, and so on, until an appropriate level of detail for the plan in question is reached.

4.6.2 Writing Product Descriptions

A Product Description should be written for a product as soon as possible after the need for the product has been identified.

A clear, complete and unambiguous description of products is a tremendous aid to their successful creation. A documented and agreed Product Description ensures that all personnel affected by that product have the same understanding. A description should be written for each significant product to ensure that it is understood, to provide a pointer to the way in which the product is to be presented, and to define the quality expectations for it.

A Product Description defines a number of things about the product:

- product title

- purpose

- composition

- derivation

- format and presentation

- quality criteria

- the method of quality check required.

Many organisations add extra information to them, such as the name of the person allocated to create the product, estimates and dates.

4.6.3 Producing a Product Flow Diagram

The Product Flow Diagram is created from the Product Breakdown Structure and shows the sequence of development of the products of the plan. It also identifies dependencies on any products outside the scope of this plan.

A Product Flow Diagram needs very few symbols. Time flows in one direction only, either from top to bottom or from left to right. Each product to be developed within the plan in question is enclosed in a box, and the boxes connected by arrows, showing the sequence in which they are to be created. Any products which should already exist or which come from work outside the scope of the plan should be clearly identified by using a different type of enclosure, e.g. an ellipse.

5.   Controls

5.1   Purpose

The purpose of control is to ensure that a project:

- produces the required products to meet the acceptance criteria defined in the project brief

- is carried out in accordance with its resource and cost plans

- traps and controls any potential change to its original specification

- remains viable against its business case.

5.1.1   Tolerance

Tolerance plays a key part in "management by exception". It is the permissible deviation from a stage or project plan without bringing the deviation to the attention of the Project Board (or higher authority if the deviation is at project level). Separate tolerance figures should be given for time and cost.

Tolerances for the project as a whole should be set by corporate or programme management in the Project Mandate (or ascertained by the Executive during Start-up and entered into the project brief). Based on these overall figures the Project Board agrees with the Project Manager a tolerance for each stage, once the stage plan has been produced.

5.2   Corporate or Programme Management Control

5.2.1   Project Mandate

The first chance of control available to senior management is the input of the Project Mandate to trigger the project. Corporate or programme management define the basic objectives, constraints, cost and time targets, acceptance criteria and business justification of the project.

5.2.2   Project Board appointment

Another point of control is the appointment of a Project Board which will carry out the requirements of senior management. Senior management appoint an appropriate Project Board Executive and have the option to appoint the whole of the Project Board, as well as the Project Manager.

5.2.3   Project Tolerance

As part of the Project Mandate, senior management have the opportunity to input their expectation of the total cost and target date of the project. They are also expected to identify to the Project Board tolerance figures which specify how much latitude the board has in meeting these figures. Any deviation outside these figures means that the Executive must refer the details and options back to them for approval before being allowed to continue with the project.

5.2.4	Reporting from the Project Board	Senior management will normally insist on a regular report from the Executive.
5.2.5	Closure Confirmation	At the end of the project the Project Board has to report back to the senior management team who appointed it on the performance of the project. This may be done by sending a copy of the End Project Report.

5.3 Project Board Control

5.3.1	Design and Appointment of the Project Management Team	The Project Board Executive and Project Manager are appointed at the outset of the project. One of their first tasks is to design the project management team. This not only covers the other members of the Project Board, but how assurance and project support will be handled.
5.3.2	Authorising Initiation	At the project initiation meeting the Project Board can review the project brief, the project approach and the initiation stage plan before deciding whether to commit the initiation resources.
5.3.3	Authorising the Project	At the end of initiation the Project Board reviews the Project Initiation Document, containing the project definition, job descriptions, project plan, business case and risk situation before deciding whether to continue with the project. If the board does decide to continue, it has to approve the next stage plan before work can go on.
5.3.4	Authorising Each Stage	At the end of each stage there is an end stage assessment where the Project Board reviews the status of the project plan, business case and risks as well as the proposed next stage plan before deciding what to do with the project.
5.3.5	Setting Stage Tolerances	As part of approving a stage plan, the Project Board give the Project Manager tolerance margins for the plan. If there is any likelihood of a deviation beyond those tolerances, the Project Manager has to advise the Project Board and ask for direction. (See the description of the exception report in the Glossary.)

5.3.6	Receiving an Exception Report	When there is a risk of exceeding the tolerance margins for either the stage or the project, the Project Manager advises the Project Board of the reason for the forecast deviation, the impact on plans, business case and risks and the options available. The Project Manager makes a recommendation and again details the impact which this would have on the plans, business case and risks. The Project Board decides what action to take.
5.3.7	Authorising an Exception Plan	In response to an exception report the Project Board will normally ask the Project Manager to raise an exception plan. This replaces the remainder of the current stage plan to fit the new situation and has to be approved by the Project Board at a Mid Stage Assessment. According to the project size and criticality this assessment may be done formally or informally. The basic purpose is for the Project Board to be aware that the situation has changed, review the impact on the project plan, the business case and the risk exposure, approve the revised plan and set new tolerances.
		If the exception report has identified a threat to the project tolerances, as opposed to the current stage tolerances, the exception plan would be for the remainder of the project, and may have to be referred upwards to corporate or programme management by the Project Board.
5.3.8	Highlight Reports	During initiation the Project Board advises the Project Manager of the frequency at which it wishes to receive progress reports, called Highlight Reports.
5.3.9	Closure Confirmation	At the end of a project the Project Manager has to prove to the Project Board that all products have been delivered and that the users and any support and maintenance functions are prepared to accept the products. The Project Board also confirms that all project issues have been closed, with any remaining action recommendations transferred to the support function.
5.4	**Project Manager Control**	
5.4.1	Work Packages	Where there is more than one team, the Project Manager and Team Managers agree on Work Packages, which describe the products to be delivered, the quality checks to be made and how the deliverables are to be approved. Target dates are also part of the packages, together with reporting requirements. Reports from

teams are checkpoint reports, and the Team Managers have to update the Quality Log with details of quality checks carried out.

5.4.2   Checkpoint Reports   Each team prepares a Checkpoint Report on a frequency defined by the Project Manager. This is normally in a similar format to the Highlight Report, and covers achievements in the period, problems and expected achievements in the next period.

5.4.3   Quality Log   The Quality Log records each quality check made, planned and actual dates, results, number of action items and sign-off date. The Project Manager refers to this as part of the control of quality work.

5.4.4   Issue Log   The Issue Log keeps track of all issues raised and their status. The Project Manager decides on the course of action to take on each issue as part of change control. Sometimes the changes requested would take the plans beyond their tolerances, and this would be one reason to trigger an exception report to the Project Board.

5.4.5   Risk Log   The Risk Log is started at the beginning of the project and it is part of the Project Manager's job to keep a regular check on the status of all identified risks. This check forms part of the control at each end stage assessment and may need to be done on a more frequent basis, depending on the project. The Project Manager can appoint "owners" of risks, people best placed to observe any change in that risk, and add activities to monitor the risks to the stage plans.

5.4.6   Stage Plan   On a day-to-day basis the Project Manager controls against the stage plan. The plan is updated based on feedback from the teams or individual members. The information is often contained in timesheets as well as the checkpoint reports. The updated plan may show if the stage is in danger of exceeding its tolerances.

5.5   **Configuration Management**   No organisation can be fully effective unless it controls and manages its assets. The assets of a project are the products which it develops. The configuration of a project is the sum total of its products. Within the context of project management the purpose of configuration management is to identify, track and protect the project's products.

Configuration management consists of four basic functions:

- **identification** – specifying and identifying all components of the final product

- **control** – the ability to agree and "freeze" configuration items and then to make changes only with the agreement of appropriate named authorities. Once a product has been approved, the motto is "Nothing moves, nothing changes without authorisation"

- **status accounting** – the recording and reporting of all current and historical data concerned with each configuration item

- **verification** – a series of reviews and audits to ensure that there is conformity between all configuration items and the authorised state of configuration items as registered in the configuration management records.

There must be a close liaison between configuration management and change control. A key element is the ability to identify and control different versions of a configuration item. Once a configuration item has been approved, that version of it never changes. If a change is required, a new version of the configuration item is created which will encompass the change. The new version should be associated with documentation of the change which caused the need for the new version.

A configuration management plan forms part of the Project Initiation Document. It consists of:

- an explanation of the purpose of configuration management

- a description of (or reference to) the configuration management method to be used

- details of any variance from corporate or department standards together with a justification for the variance

- reference to any other configuration management systems with which links will be necessary

- the name of the Configuration Librarian

- identification of the products or classes of product which will be configuration items

- a plan of what libraries, files and other locations will be used to hold configuration items

- confirmation that the relevant project and stage files have been set up.

6. Stages

6.1	**What is a Stage?**	Stages are parts of a project with decision points. A stage is a collection of activities and products whose delivery is managed as a unit. As such it is a sub-set of the project, and in PRINCE 2 terms it is the element of work which the Project Manager is managing on behalf of the Project Board at any one time. The use of stages in a PRINCE 2 project is mandatory. The number of stages is flexible and depends on the needs of the project.
6.2	**Why are Stages Important?**	The division of a project into stages is an important control for the Project Board. The Project Board's commitment is limited to only the current stage, at the end of which it can get an update on the status of the business case and risks as well as a view of the next stage plan before deciding whether to commit to the next stage.

The breakdown of a project into stages allows the Project Board to "manage by exception". It gives the Project Manager authority to get on with a stage. By setting tolerance levels the Project Board knows that it will get warning of any potential deviation beyond these tolerances and a chance to re-direct the project without the need for regular progress meetings.

The concept of stages is important to the Project Manager in that it allows detailed planning of only as much of the project as can be done with confidence, and reduces the planning work at the beginning of a project. Each part of the project is only planned in detail immediately before that part of the project is about to start, thus allowing the Project Manager to gain as much information about it as possible from the work which has gone on before.

Every project should consist of at least two stages. A small project may need only two stages; an initiation stage and the remainder of the project in the second stage. For a small project, the initiation stage may last only a matter of hours, but is essential to ensure that there is a firm basis for the project, understood by all parties.

The main reasons for breaking a project into stages are summarised as follows.

6.2.1 Review and Decision Points

Where a project lasts for more than a few weeks there may be a need to limit commitment to only the current part of the project, at which time the Project Board can review the continuing viability of the project and make decisions on further commitments.

PRINCE 2 uses stages to deal with these decision points. The decisions and the information on which they are based form the basis of the end stage assessments. The benefits these end stage assessments bring to the project are:

- providing a "fire break" for the project by encouraging the Project Board to assess the project viability at regular intervals, rather than let it run on in an uncontrolled manner

- ensuring that key decisions are made prior to the detailed work needed to implement them

- clarifying what the impact will be of an identified external influence such as the corporate budget round or the finalisation of legislation.

6.2.2 Planning Horizons

Uncertainty can often mean that it is only possible to plan in detail the activities and products of a limited amount of the work of the project. The rest of the project's work can only be planned in broad outline. The adoption of stages handles this situation by having two different but related levels of plan, i.e. a detailed stage plan and an outline project plan.

6.2.3 Scale

Most projects need to be broken down into more manageable stages to enable the correct level of planning and control to be exercised.

6.3 **How to Define Stages**

The process of defining stages is fundamentally a process of balancing:

- how far ahead in a project it is sensible to plan in detail

- where the key decision points need to be on a project

- too many small stages versus too few big ones.

This will be a balance of the factors identified above, and will be influenced by any team plans. However, the Project Manager will have to reconcile the stage plan and any associated team plans.

6.4   How to Use Stages

There are several factors to consider when choosing the number of stages for a project; the exposure of the project to risks (and any key moments when these may change), the duration of the project, the products whose development will cause a large outlay of resources, the uncertainty about some future aspect of the work.

The PRINCE 2 technique of product-based planning is invaluable here since by using it the Project Manager can identify all the products which are due to be produced within any given stage. This can then be used to assess completion or otherwise of the stage.

7.   Management of Risk

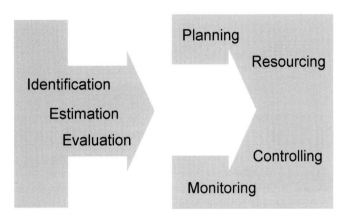

Risk Analysis   **Risk Management**

Figure 6: Risk Analysis and Risk Management

| 7.1 | **Purpose** | Risk can be defined as: |

"the chance of exposure to the adverse consequences of future events".

By their nature projects are set up to deal with change, and hence the future is less predictable than is typically the case with routine work. In addition, projects can be large and complex, and can be dealing with novel or unusual factors. As such risk is a major factor to be considered during the management of a project.

| 7.2 | **Types of Risk** | In PRINCE 2 there are broadly two types of risk: |

- business risk; this covers the threats to a project not achieving its benefits

- project risk; this is the collection of threats to the management of the project and hence the achievement of the project's objectives within cost and time; these will be many and varied, but would include external factors (i.e. factors that are outside the control of the project).

It must be stressed that risks to each project must be considered in their own right.

| 7.3 | **The Management of Risk** | In order to contain the risks during a project, they must be managed in a structured manner. This structure consists of two phases: |

- risk analysis, which involves the identification and definition of risks

- risk management, which covers the activities involved in the planning, monitoring and controlling of actions which will address the threats and problems identified, so as to improve the likelihood of the project achieving its stated objectives.

7.3.1   Risk Analysis

Risk analysis is an essential prerequisite to effective risk management. It comprises three activities:

- risk identification, which lists all the potential risks that could be faced by a project

- risk estimation, which determines how important each risk is, based on an assessment of its likelihood, and consequences to the project and business

- risk evaluation, which decides whether the level of each risk is acceptable or not and, if not, what actions can be taken to make it more acceptable.

The results of the risk analysis activities will be documented in the Risk Log.

These risk analysis activities are overlapping, with many iterations involved. Risk analysis is a process which will be conducted continuously throughout the project as information becomes available, and as circumstances change. However, there is a need to carry out a major risk analysis at the start of the project and at the end of each stage.

7.3.2   Risk Management

Once the risks have been identified and evaluated, attention needs to focus on managing them. Risk management logically follows risk analysis, though, as with analysis, the two phases may overlap.

Risks can be transferred to others (e.g. insurance or sub-contracting). Where they remain with the project, risk management consists of four major activities:

- planning

- resourcing

- monitoring

- controlling.

As with any management process, risk management will be done continuously throughout the project. However, there will be certain points in the project management cycle where actions will need to be carried out.

Risk planning and resourcing will be done in the "Planning" process and control will be carried out during "Controlling a Stage".

8. Quality in a Project Environment

8.1 What is Quality?

Quality is defined in ISO 8402 (BS4778) as "the totality of features and characteristics of a product or service which bear on its ability to satisfy stated needs."

Interpreting this into more practical definitions, quality is the production of products and services which:

- are fit for their purpose
- conform to their requirements
- are designed and produced to do the job properly
- meet customer requirements.

One of these will be appropriate for different product types. Within projects, quality is a question of identifying what it is about the project's products or services which makes them fit for the purpose of satisfying stated needs.

8.2 Quality Management

Quality management is the process of ensuring that the quality expected by the customer is achieved. It encompasses all the project management activities which determine the project's quality plan, and implement it. The various elements of an organisation's quality management interrelate and are as follows:

- A *Quality System* with an organisation structure, procedures and processes to implement quality management. Both the customer and the supplier may have quality systems. The project may have to use one of these quality systems or an agreed mixture of both. PRINCE 2 itself will typically form part of a corporate quality system where it has been adopted as a corporate standard.

- *Quality Assurance* which sets up the quality system and is the means of assuring that the quality system operates to achieve an end product that meets quality and customer requirements. It creates and maintains the quality system, audits and evaluates it. A quality assurance function may be set up separate from and independent of the organisation's project and operational activities to monitor use of the quality system across all projects within the corporate body. If such an independent body does not exist,

45

the project assurance function within the project will assume the quality assurance role.

- *Quality Planning* which establishes the objectives and requirements for quality and lays out the activities for the application of the quality system. In the Project Initiation Document the quality approach for the whole project is defined under "Project Quality Plan". It is important that the customer's quality expectations are understood and documented prior to project commencement. Each stage plan specifies in detail the required quality activities and resources, with the detailed quality criteria shown in the Product Descriptions.

- *Quality Control* which is the means of ensuring that products meet the quality criteria specified for them. Quality control is about examining products to determine that they meet requirements.

8.3   The PRINCE 2 Approach to Quality

The approach in PRINCE 2 to the provision of quality products is illustrated in Figure 7.

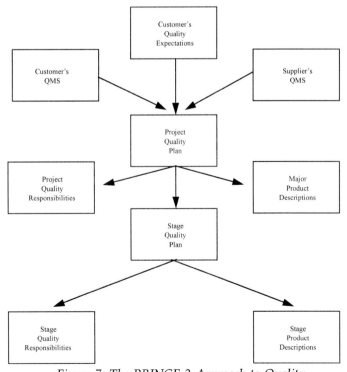

Figure 7: The PRINCE 2 Approach to Quality

8.3.1	The Customer's Quality Expectations	The customer's quality expectations should be made clear in the Project Mandate at the very outset of the project. If not sufficiently clear, the Project Manager should clarify the expectations when preparing the project brief (during "Start Up the Project" (SU)). The expectations should be measurable. "Of good quality" may sound fine, but is difficult to measure. Expectations of performance, reliability, flexibility, maintainability and capability should all be expressed in measurable terms.

Not every product needs to be of top quality in every respect. Not every product is required to be beautifully polished, easy-to-use and capable of working for ever. There are products which are designed to be thrown away after one use, other products where early availability of the product is far more important than ease-of-use, flexibility or maintainability.

The customer has to decide where the project's main focus is to be. Does it incline more towards the cost, the time or the quality? The three items are inter-linked. If you want the product to be cheap, that may have an adverse effect on the quality, and so on.

8.3.2 The Project Quality Plan

The next step is to decide how the project is going to meet the customer's quality expectations for the product. This is done as part of the process "Initiating a Project" (IP). Other inputs to this should be the Project Approach (designed in process "Starting up a Project" (SU)), the standards to be used to guide the development of the product and test its ability to meet the quality expectations. The supplier should have standards, but the customer may also have standards which it insists on being used. Such standards have to be compared against the expectations to see which are to be used. There may be gaps where extra standards have to be obtained or created. The customer has the last say in what standards will be used to check the products.

The project quality plan identifies the standards to be used and the main quality responsibilities. The latter may be a reference to a Quality Assurance function (belonging to either the customer, the supplier or both). There is a cross-reference here to the Project Board roles. These roles contain assurance responsibilities, some of them affecting quality. If these have been delegated, there must be a match between job descriptions and the responsibilities defined in the project quality plan.

The project quality plan refers to the establishment of the Quality Log, the Quality File and their purposes. The plan also identifies the procedures which will be used to control changes and the configuration management plan.

8.3.3 The Stage Quality Plan

Each stage has its own quality plan containing lower level detail than the project quality plan. This identifies the method of quality checking to be used for each product of the stage.

The plan also identifies responsibilities for each individual quality check. For example, for each Quality Review the Chairman and Reviewers should be identified. This gives an opportunity for those with assurance responsibility to see each draft stage plan and input their needs for checking and the staff who should represent it at each check.

Any major products developed in the stage should have Product Descriptions written for them, if they were not done as part of the project quality plan.

8.4 The Quality Log

The Quality Log records details of how each product is to be checked, the quality checking method to be used, responsibilities, results and dates.

There is only one Quality Log per project, even if there are several teams. All Team Managers, including sub-contractors must provide details of checks made to the central Quality Log. It can then provide an audit trail of all quality checking done and also act as a reference point for the Project Manager to check on quality work.

8.5 Quality Review

PRINCE 2 offers a Quality Review technique, which is an effective way to check on the quality of any document. A Quality Review is a team review of a product with the emphasis on checking the product for errors (as opposed to, for example, improving the product's design).

A Quality Review can be invoked at any point in the project, since any document could be subject to a Quality Review if there are subjective elements of quality to be monitored. It has close ties with the following processes:

- "Planning" (PL) for the pre-planning and resourcing of major Quality Reviews

- "Managing Product Delivery" (MP) which is the process covering the production of the project's products, and hence where the application of most of the Quality Reviews will take place

- "Controlling a Stage" (CS) which addresses the hand-over of responsibility for product production which will include the requirement for Quality Reviews, and also deals with progress monitoring and reporting, and which will receive details of completed Quality Reviews.

8.5.1 Objectives

The objectives of a Quality Review are:

- to ensure that a product will meet business, user and specialist requirements

- to assess the conformity of a product against set criteria

- to provide a platform for product improvement

- to involve all those who have a vested interest in the product

- to spread ownership of the product

- to obtain commitment from all vested interests in the product

- to provide a mechanism for management control.

8.5.2 Steps in the Quality Review Procedure

There are three basic steps in the Quality Review technique.

- Preparation, consisting of:

  - confirmation of the availability of the nominated reviewers and agreement on dates for the return of comments and the review itself

  - distribution of a copy of the product and its Product Description to Reviewers where this is possible, for instance, if it is a printed document. Alternatively, making the product available for inspection by the Reviewers

  - assessment of the product against the quality criteria

  - entry of the major errors on an Error List

- annotation of minor errors on the product, where applicable
- return of the annotated product and Error List to the Producer
- a plan of the review meeting, and agreement on the agenda.

- Review Meeting, consisting of:
  - discussion and clarification of each of the major errors raised by the Reviewers
  - agreement of the follow-up appropriate to each error
  - documentation of the follow-up actions and responsibilities
  - summary of the actions at the end of the meeting
  - agreement on the Quality Review outcome, and sign-off of the product, if appropriate.

- Follow-up, consisting of:
  - notification to the Team Manager of Quality Review results
  - a plan of any remedial work required
  - sign-off of the product following successful remedial work.

9. Change Control

Every project is subject to changes of some kind. Lack of control over these changes will destroy any chance of bringing the project in on schedule, to budget and specification.

A project therefore needs a method of controlling changes and their effect on the project. This technique must make sure they are not ignored, but that nothing is implemented of which the appropriate level of management is unaware. This includes the Project Board. In PRINCE 2 all possible changes are handled as Project Issues. Apart from controlling possible changes, this provides a formal entry point through which all points can be raised. There are three types of Project Issue in PRINCE 2:

- Enquiry/Complaint
- Requests For Change
- Off-Specifications.

9.1 The Issue Log

All three types of issue are logged on one central Issue Log. This is used to allocate a unique reference to each issue and keep track of its status.

9.2 Enquiry/Complaint

A Project Issue is the formal way into a project of any enquiry or complaint. It can be raised by anyone associated with the project about anything. There is no limit to the content of a Project Issue beyond the fact that it should be about the project.

Normally, after analysis, an enquiry or complaint can be answered directly, after which it is closed.

9.3 Request For Change

A Request For Change records a proposed modification to the established user requirements. It requires analysis to see how much work is involved. It is particularly important to identify any already accepted products which would need to be changed, because changes to such items must be approved by the Project Board as part of its control.

The identified work is costed and the impact on the stage plan's budget and schedule assessed, as well as any potential impact on the business case and the risks. If the work to do the Request For Change cannot be done within the tolerance levels of the current stage plan, the decision on action must come from the Project Board. The Project Manager must submit an exception report. (This is described in the process "Controlling a Stage" (CS).)

9.4   Off-Specification

An Off-Specification is used to document any situation where the product or project is failing to meet its specification in some respect.

If the Off-Specification does not involve a change to a product which has already been accepted and the work can be done within the current plan's tolerances, the Project Manager can make the decision to implement it. If the Off-Specification requires changes to one or more products which the Project Board has already been told are complete (to any baseline, not necessarily the final one), or if the work to do the Off-Specification cannot be done within the tolerance levels of the stage plan, the decision must be made by the Project Board. The Project Manager must submit an exception report to the Project Board.

10. Version 1 and 2 Differences

This chapter is for those people who have experience of the first version of PRINCE and who wish to know what changes have been made to the method. This document lists the changes and describes them, together with the reasoning behind the changes.

10.1 IT References Removed

All IT references have been removed. PRINCE 2 is a project management method for **any** type of project. In Version 1 there was an overlap between PRINCE and SSADM, the CCTA recommended set of analysis and design techniques for computer projects. All such references have now been removed.

10.2 Customer/Supplier Environment

PRINCE 1 was written assuming that the project management team would all come from within the same organisation. The method is now written from a customer/supplier viewpoint. This means that the method assumes that the customer with the problem and the supplier of the solution may have separate managements. Other scenarios are covered, but the main bulk of the method is written from this basis. Even where one department is producing a solution for another department within the same company, increasingly these are treated as separate cost centres and therefore fit naturally into a customer/supplier environment.

10.3 Suitability for Small Projects

There is a great deal of emphasis in PRINCE 2 on deciding how formal or informal information-passing and decision-making needs to be, based on the individual project's needs. In many cases, the method now suggests that information can be exchanged and decisions taken without the need for formal documents and/or meetings.

The Organisation component, for example, puts the assurance responsibilities in the role descriptions for the Project Board members, and suggests that only if the project warrants it should the work of assurance be delegated to others.

10.4 Processes

If we think about ISO 9001, we can recognise that it requires each process in the production of a product to be documented. As part of closer alignment with the needs of ISO 9001, therefore, the "steps" to take in project management within PRINCE 2 are defined in a series of processes. These are outlined in Chapter 2.

10.5   Organisation

Assurance is now more clearly identified as a Project Board responsibility. The work of assurance can be delegated to assurance people (the old co-ordinators) if, for example, the size or complexity of the project suggest this. This is to avoid small project members feeling that the use of PRINCE 2 would need too much overhead, and reinforces the Project Board's responsibilities as "owner" of the project. It also emphasises the independence of assurance, describes the potential link with any independent Quality Assurance function and gets away from the PRINCE 1 practice, where the Project Assurance Team (PAT) had become part of the Project Manager's team, e.g. the Business Assurance Co-ordinator (BAC) often being involved in the creation and update of plans. This was thought to have destroyed the independence of the assurance function, which is correspondingly upgraded.

The Stage Manager role name has been changed to Team Manager. According to the views of PRINCE 1 users, very little use was being made of the Stage Manager role in its pure sense, but very often a Project Manager would find him- or herself controlling work via a number of teams. There was also the need to deal with the environment where the Project Manager was part of the customer's organisation, but much of the work was being done by contractors. It was felt that the name of Team Manager was more flexible and applicable to more project organisation situations.

Project Support has been brought back as administrative support to the Project Manager where needed. This is to absorb those jobs often done by members of the PAT which were felt to affect their independence and, hence, their capability to carry out assurance on behalf of the Project Board.

10.6   Risk Management

This is not a new topic, but risk gets much more exposure in PRINCE 2. There is now a Risk Log, a component chapter on Risk in the manual and the processes also stress the need to review all risks throughout the project. The method stresses that its approach to risk is compatible with the CCTA published guidance on Management of Risk.

10.7 Project Exceptions

There is now more emphasis on the Project Manager **forecasting** a deviation beyond tolerances, rather than reacting to a deviation which has already happened. The interface is an exception report which contains the text which used to be part of the exception plan, namely:

- problem

- options

- impact on business case and risks

- recommendation.

The Project Board response to an exception report will normally be to ask the Project Manager to raise an exception plan. This now has a format like any other PRINCE 2 plan. An exception plan is presented at a mid stage assessment. All of the other purposes for a mid stage assessment in PRINCE 1 have been dropped, i.e. there is no mid stage assessment in the middle of a long stage. It is now strongly recommended to break the stage into two or more shorter stages.

10.8 Technical

The term is dropped, mainly because there was a tie in to IT terminology with the constant use of "technical". "Senior Technical" becomes "Senior Supplier", "Technical Exceptions" are now "Project Issues". The separation of technical and resource plans is no longer made. As most people use a piece of software as a planning tool which can generate both types of report from the one plan, the old distinction was felt to be unnecessary.

10.9 Quality

The Quality Review is still there, but it is pointed out that it is only one type of quality check. A Quality Log is introduced to keep a record of **all** quality checks done.

10.10 ISO 9001

There is a much closer relationship between PRINCE 2 and ISO 9001. PRINCE 2 does not meet all the requirements of the quality standard, because a number of the ISO standards apply to an entire site or company, rather than an individual project. An Appendix in the PRINCE 2 manual describes the sections of ISO 9001 and relates PRINCE 2 to each one.

10.11 Plans

The individual work plan is dropped because it never was a real plan, simply an extract from a stage or detailed plan. The detailed plan is now called a team plan.

The three levels of plan are retained; project, stage and team. Mainly for the benefit of small projects, it is emphasised that the project plan is the only mandatory plan.

The product-based planning technique is retained.

10.12 Stages

There is a separate section in the PRINCE 2 manual to explain stages, though there is no difference in their concept to PRINCE 1.

10.13 Products

PRINCE 2 is still product-based. The PRINCE 2 manual gives Product Outlines for all management products. A Product Outline is a Product Description without "Format", "Quality Method" or "Responsible" sections. Tailoring is needed to turn an outline into a Product Description. In line with the method's move away from its former IT concentration, the Product Descriptions for technical products are no longer offered.

10.14 Programme Management

There is now a firm link between projects and programmes. Programmes are explained, together with their relationships to projects. Throughout the method there are reminders of the possible impact of programme decisions on projects and vice versa.

11. Glossary

Term	Definition
Acceptance Criteria	A prioritised list of criteria which the final product(s) must meet before the customer will accept them. They should be defined as part of the project brief and agreed between customer and supplier no later than the Project Initiation stage. They should be in the Project Initiation Document.
Baseline	A snapshot; a position or situation which is recorded. Although the position may be updated later, the baseline remains unchanged and available as a reminder of the original state and as a comparison against the current position.
Business Case	Information which describes the justification for setting up and continuing a PRINCE 2 project. It provides the reasons (answers the question "why?") for the project. It is updated at key points throughout the project.
Change Authority	A group to which the Project Board may delegate responsibility for the consideration of Requests For Change. The Change Authority is given a budget and can approve changes within that budget.
Change Budget	The money allocated to the Change Authority to be spent on authorised Requests For Change.
Change Control	The procedure to ensure that the processing of all Project Issues is controlled, including the submission, analysis and decision making.
Checkpoint	A team level, time-driven review of progress.
Checkpoint Report	A progress report of the information gathered at a Checkpoint meeting, which is sent from a team to the Project Manager, and provides reporting data as defined in the Project Initiation Document.
Concession	An Off-Specification which is accepted by the Project Board without corrective action.

Term	Definition
Configuration Management	A discipline, normally supported by software tools, which gives management precise control over its assets (e.g. the products of a project), covering identification, control, status accounting and verification of the products.
Contingency Plan	A plan which provides an outline of decisions and measures to be taken if defined circumstances, outside the control of a PRINCE 2 project, should occur.
Corporate and corporate body	Used to describe any company, government department, corporation, charitable body, which is involved in a project. It can be a customer for the end results, supplier of specialist skills or deliverables, assurance or auditing body. The word is used to avoid confusion particularly between the public and private sectors.
Customer	The person or group who commissioned the work.
Deliverable(s)	An item which the project has to create as part of the requirements. It may be part of the final outcome or an intermediate element on which one or more subsequent deliverables are dependent. According to the type of project, another name for a deliverable would be "product".
End Project Report	A report sent from the Project Manager to the Project Board, which confirms the hand-over of all deliverables, provides an updated business case, and an assessment of how well the project has done against its Project Initiation Document.
End Stage Assessment	The review by the Project Board and Project Manager at the end of a stage of the End Stage Report to decide whether to approve the next stage plan (unless the last stage has now been completed). According to the size and criticality of the project, the review may be formal or informal. The approval to proceed should be documented as an important management product.

Term	Definition
End Stage Report	A report sent by the Project Manager to the Project Board at the end of each management stage of a PRINCE 2 project. This provides information about the project performance during the stage and the project status at stage end.
Exception	A situation where it can be forecast that there will be a deviation beyond the tolerance levels agreed between Project Manager and Project Board or between Project Board and corporate or programme management.
Exception Plan	A plan which follows an exception report. For a stage or team plan exception it covers the period from the present to the end of the current stage. If the exception is at a project level, the project plan would be revised.
Exception Report	A report which describes an exception, provides an analysis and options for the way forward and identifies a recommended option. It is sent from the Project Manager to the Project Board.
Executive	The chairman of the Project Board, representing the customer.
Follow-On Action Recommendations	A report which can be used as input to the process of creating a business case/project mandate for any follow-on PRINCE 2 project, and/or for recording any follow-on instructions covering incomplete products or outstanding issues. It also sets out proposals for post implementation review of the project's deliverables.
Highlight Report	Report from the Project Manager to the Project Board on a time-driven frequency on stage progress.
Issue Log	A log of all issues and change requests raised during the project, showing details of each issue, its evaluation, what decisions about it have been made and its current status.

Term	Definition
Lessons Learned Report	A report which describes the lessons learned in undertaking a PRINCE 2 project and which includes statistics from the quality control of the project's management products. It is approved by the Project Board then held centrally for the benefit of future projects.
Off-Specification	Something which should be provided by the project, but currently is not (or is forecast not to be provided). This might be a missing product or a product not meeting its specification.
PIM	*see* Project Initiation Meeting.
Post Implementation Review	One or more reviews held after project closure to determine if the expected benefits have been obtained.
PRINCE	A method which supports some selected aspects of project management. The acronym stands for *Projects in Controlled Environments*.
PRINCE 2 Project	A project whose deliverable(s) can be defined at its start sufficiently precisely as to be measurable against pre-defined metrics and which is managed according to the PRINCE 2 method.
Process	That which must be done to bring about a particular outcome, in terms of information to be gathered, decisions to be made and results which must be achieved.
Producer	This role represents the creator(s) of a document which is the subject of a Quality Review. Typically it will be filled by the person who has produced the product, or who led the team responsible.
Product	Any output from a project. PRINCE 2 distinguishes between management products (which are produced as part of the management of the project), specialist products (which are those products which make up the final deliverable) and quality products (which are produced for or by the quality process). A product may itself be a collection of other products.
Product Breakdown Structure	A hierarchy of all the products to be produced during a plan.

Term	Definition
Product Description	A description of a product's purpose, composition, derivation and quality criteria. It is produced at planning time, as soon as the need for the product is identified.
Product Flow Diagram	A diagram showing the sequence of production and interdependencies of the products listed in a Product Breakdown Structure.
Project	A temporary organisation which is created for the purpose of delivering one or more business products according to a specified business case.
Project Assurance	The Project Board's responsibilities to assure itself that the project is being conducted correctly.
Project Brief	A description of what the project is to do; a refined and extended version of the Project Mandate, which has been agreed by the Project Board and which is input to Project Initiation.
Project Closure Notification	Advice from the Project Manager to inform the host location that the project resources can be disbanded and support services, such as space, equipment and access, released.
Project Initiation Document	A logical document whose purpose is to bring together the key information needed to start the project on a sound basis; and to convey that information to all concerned with the project.
Project Initiation Meeting	The meeting for the "DP" process "Authorising Initiation". It is the first meeting of the Project Board. It occurs after "Starting Up a Project" and triggers the Initiation stage.
Project Issue	A term used to cover both general issues and change requests raised during the project. Project Issues can be about anything to do with the project. They cover questions, suggestions, Requests For Change and Off-Specification.
Project Management	The planning, monitoring and control of all aspects of a project and the motivation of all those involved in it to achieve the project objectives on time and to the specified cost, quality and performance.

Term	Definition
Project Management Team	A term to represent the entire management structure of Project Board, Project Manager, plus any Team Managers and project assurance roles.
Project Manager	The person given the authority and responsibility to manage the project on a day-to-day basis to deliver the required products within the constraints agreed with the Project Board.
Project Mandate	A document, created externally to the project, which forms the terms of reference and is used to start-up a PRINCE 2 project.
Project Plan	A high-level plan showing the major products of the project, when they will be delivered and at what cost. An initial project plan is presented as part of the Project Initiation Document. This is revised in later versions as information on actual progress appears. It is a major control document for the Project Board to measure actual progress against expectations.
Project Quality Plan	The definition of key quality criteria and quality control and audit processes to be applied to project management and technical work in the PRINCE 2 project. It will be part of the text in the Project Initiation Document.
Project Records	A collection of all approved management, specialist and quality products and other material, which is necessary to provide an auditable record of a PRINCE 2 project. NB. This does **not** include working files.
Project Start-up Notification	Advice to the host location that the project is about to start and requesting any required project support services.
Project Support Office	A group set up to provide certain administrative services to the Project Manager. Often the group provides its services to many projects.
Quality	The totality of features and characteristics of a product or service which bear on its ability to satisfy stated and implied needs.

Term	Definition
Quality Management System	The complete set of quality standards, procedures and responsibilities for a site or organisation.
Quality Review	A Quality Review is an inspection with a specific structure, defined roles and procedure designed to ensure a document's completeness and adherence to standards. The participants are drawn from those with an interest in the document and those with the necessary skills to review its correctness. An example of the checks made by a Quality Review is "does the document match the Quality Criteria in the Product Description?"
Quality System	*see* Quality Management System
Request For Change	A means of proposing a modification to the current specification of the product required. It is one type of Project Issue.
Reviewer	A person asked to check a product for errors or omissions at a Quality Review.
Risk Log	A document which provides identification, estimation, impact evaluation and counter-measures for all risks to a PRINCE 2 project. It should initially be created at the outset of the project and be developed during the life of the project.
Risk Report	A report which records and describes any development which poses a risk to a PRINCE 2 project.
Senior User	A member of the Project Board, accountable for ensuring that user needs are specified correctly and that the solution meets those needs.
Stage	A division of the project for management purposes. The Project Board approve the project to proceed one stage at a time.
Supplier	Supplier is defined as the group or groups responsible for the supply of a project's products.
Tolerance	The permissible deviation above and below a plan's estimate of time and cost without escalating the deviation to the next level of management. Separate tolerance figures should be given for time and cost.

Term	Definition
User(s)	The person or group who will use the final deliverable(s) of the project.
Work Package	The set of information relevant to the creation of one or more products. It will contain the Product Description(s), details of any constraints on production such as time and cost, interfaces, and confirmation of the agreement between the Project Manager and the person or Team Manager who is to implement the Work Package that the work can be done within the constraints.
Work Package Authorisation	Authority from the Project Manager to produce a defined Work Package.

Printed in the United Kingdom for The Stationery Office
TJ 002384 09/00 C13 10170